Fundamentals of "21"

By
Mason Malmuth and Lynne Loomis

A product of Two Plus Two Publishing

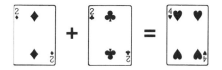

THIRD EDITION
First Printing
May 2004

Printing and Binding
Creel Printing Co.
Las Vegas, Nevada

Printed in the United States of America

Fundamentals of "21"

For information contact: **Two Plus Two Publishing, LLC**
600 West Sunset
Suite 103
Henderson, NV 89015
(702) 896-1326
www.twoplustwo.com

ISBN: 1-880685-29-9

Dedicated to the Memory of

Walter I. Nolan
(1924-1987)

*Walter I. Nolan, whose initials form the acronym
WIN, was the pen name of the late John Luckman,
the founder of Gambler's Book Club. During his
illustrious career, Luckman not only wrote numerous
books and pamphlets on various gambling topics,
but also was directly responsible for bringing to
life many additional top-quality works by other gaming
authors. He is remembered for his integrity, his
adherence to high standards, and his devotion
to both the publishing and gaming industries.*

*It was with the hope of following the tradition
established by John Luckman that the* Fundamentals
of "21" *was written, and it is with honor and
reverence that this booklet is dedicated to the
memory of his literary pseudonym, Walter I. Nolan.*

Table of Contents

Introduction

The game of blackjack — formally known as "21" — is the most widely played table game offered by casinos. And no wonder. Blackjack is exciting, the action is fast and furious, and though a great deal of luck is involved in the short run, a knowledgeable player actually can attain an edge over the casino, which is the primary allure of this game.

The *Fundamentals of "21"* covers some of the concepts that will enable you, in certain situations, to gain an advantage over the house. However, prior to discussing these ideas, we will describe how the game is played, outline the customary procedures used at the "21" tables, and provide guidelines that will make it possible for you to reduce the house advantage to an acceptable minimum.

This manual has been written for the novice player who would like to have a reasonable gamble when he visits a casino and for the social player who would like to improve his skills. It is not aimed at the player who is trying to achieve expert status. Imparting the extensive knowledge necessary to become an expert player is beyond the scope of the *Fundamentals of "21."* However, mastering the concepts in this booklet will get you started on the path toward skilled play and will enable you to obtain better results than the majority of people who sit down at the "21" tables.

Should you decide at some future time to seriously pursue the game of blackjack on a more advanced level, you will find the material listed in the "Recommended Reading" section of this manual essential to your success.

A Brief History

The origin of "21" is unknown, but it has been around for a long time. Vingt-et-un (French for "21") has been popular in Europe for several centuries, and the game was widely played in the gambling halls of the Old West. Blackjack also was featured in the early days of Las Vegas gambling, but in the 1930s, it didn't enjoy the popularity of craps and roulette. A primary reason was that blackjack couldn't be beat, and most people who played the game lost their money very rapidly. But this unhappy situation was destined to change.

In 1956, an article by Roger Baldwin, Wilbert Cantey, Herbert Maisel, and James McDermott was published in the *Journal of the American Statistical Association*. The article was an incredible breakthrough for blackjack players, since a reasonably correct basic strategy — an accurate method of play based on a player's cards and the dealer's upcard — was presented.

Unfortunately, the information furnished by the four mathematicians received little interest or publicity. But one man who did notice was Edward O. Thorp, a young physics professor at MIT. Thorp wrote a computer program that could analyze blackjack at high speed, and he ultimately devised a way to beat the game. His book, *Beat the Dealer*, caused a sensation when it was published in 1962. So much so, in fact, that the casinos altered their rules. However, when play dropped off dramatically in a short period of time, the original rules were quickly reinstated.

Thorp's book not only created winning "21" players but also immensely popularized the game. Blackjack was now known to be a "good gamble," and everyone wanted to play it. Before long, it would become the most popular and widely available casino table game.

As the years have gone by, numerous refinements to Thorp's original strategy have appeared, along with many excellent books on the game of blackjack. A most notable refinement was the development of point counts, which were much simpler to use than Thorp's original Ten count. As a result, if a player could add and subtract the number 1, he could learn to count cards proficiently with only a fair amount of practice. The blackjack revolution was now under way in earnest, and there would be no turning back.

The Basics of "21"

Today's Player

Blackjack players fall into four categories. The first is the typical visitor to a gambling center, a novice player who is attracted to the game because of its popularity, its appearance of simplicity, and its promise of a good gamble. Even though he lacks knowledge and experience, the novice player doesn't really do too badly at blackjack. Peter Griffin, a math professor at Cal State Sacramento, has shown that with favorable rules, the house advantage over a typical tourist is only 1.5 percent to 2 percent — not very big when compared to some of the other casino games.[1] Nevertheless, since a lot of hands can be played in a short period of time, this small house edge can quickly add up to a large sum of money.

The second category is the basic strategist, a player who knows the correct decisions to make based on his cards and the dealer's upcard. In most casinos, the basic strategy player will be at a slight disadvantage to the house — usually no more than 0.5 percent. Occasionally, however, a casino will offer a single-deck game with such favorable rules that someone who utilizes perfect basic strategy will have a small edge over the house.

(We need to mention that there are some players who think they understand basic strategy but really don't. In most cases, these people don't do much better than the typical visitor to a gambling center. So when we discuss basic strategy, make sure you learn and understand it completely.)

Then there's the third category of player, the card counter. An expert card counter who plays perfect basic strategy can have as

---

[1] Sadly, Professor Griffin passed away in 1999.

much as a 1.5 percent edge over the house. But to obtain an advantage this large, a player not only must be highly skilled, but also must be able to find a very good game. In fact, achieving an edge this big is rare, but opportunities still appear on occasion.

The fourth category of player is a person who uses other advantage techniques to gain an edge over the house. Some of these methods are shuffle tracking, sequencing, and front loading. These techniques are beyond the scope of this book, but there is some discussion of them in the recommended reading.

The Game

The object of blackjack is to make a total higher than the dealer's total without going over 21. If your total exceeds 21 — that is, if you bust — you lose even if the dealer also goes over 21. This is the casino's main advantage. Since you must act first, you can lose regardless of what the dealer does.

But you also have some advantages. In most casinos, you have the options of splitting pairs and of doubling down on certain hands. These options allow you to put more money on the table in favorable situations and, when used properly, can be very advantageous. In addition, when you are dealt a blackjack — an ace and a 10-value card — you will get paid three units for every two units that you've bet.[2]

A typical casino blackjack game is played using anywhere from one deck to eight decks of cards. (Games using three decks, five decks, and seven decks of cards are seldom, if ever, seen, although there is no reason why an odd number of decks could not be used.) Single- and double-deck games are generally dealt by

---

[2] Some casinos today are paying only 6-to-5 on blackjacks in their single-deck games. As you will see later, this rule is very disadvantageous for the player.

hand, whereas games using a larger number of decks are dealt from a wooden (or plastic) box called a "shoe."

All cards are assigned their rank values, with the exception of face cards and aces. Face cards carry a value of 10, and an ace — at the player's option — is worth either 1 or 11 (although an ace cannot be counted as 11 if it puts a player over 21).

As already noted, if the first two cards dealt to you are an ace and either a ten or a face card, you have a blackjack — also known as a "natural" — and will receive a 3-to-2 payoff. If the dealer has a blackjack and you don't, you will lose your original bet. If both you and the dealer have a blackjack, a tie is declared and no money changes hands.

Should you be dealt two cards of the same rank, you have the option to split your pair. That is, you may separate your cards into two hands and put up an additional amount of money equal to your original bet. You will receive cards on both hands, which you now play against the dealer. Most casinos will allow you to split again if you catch another card of the same rank. The exception is aces, which in most houses can be split only once. In addition, when you split a pair of aces, you will receive only one additional card on each hand.

If you do not have the option of splitting, you may be permitted to double down — post an additional amount of money equal to your original bet — on certain hands. When you exercise this option, you will receive only one more card. Most casinos in Las Vegas allow doubling down on any first two cards, but some houses restrict this option to only those hands in which the first two cards total either 10 or 11.

If you don't split or double down, you will have the option to hit or to stand. That is, either you may ask for additional cards — as long as your total is not over 21 — or you may declare that you do not want any more cards. When you are satisfied with your hand — assuming, of course, that you don't bust — the dealer will play out his hand, then will compare his total to your total. You win if the dealer busts or if your total is closer to 21 than his; the dealer wins if you bust or if his total is closer to 21 than yours. If both you and the dealer have the same total, no money changes hands. This is known as a "push."

At the Table

The game of "21" is played at a semicircular table that seats six or seven players. Also present will be the house dealer. After making your buy-in and placing the number of chips you wish to wager in your betting space, you will receive your first two cards.

Depending on the game, your first two cards will be dealt either face up or face down. Single- and double-deck games are generally dealt face down, while in most shoe games, the cards are distributed face up.

In a face-down game, you are permitted to lift your cards slightly above the table surface in order to see them and determine their total. If you are satisfied with your hand — that is, you wish to stand pat — slide your cards face down beneath your chips in the betting space.

 **STAND PAT**

If you want another card, when it is your turn to act, pick up your two cards and scrape them toward you on the felt in one or two quick motions. This will indicate to the dealer that you want a "hit," and he will then give you a card face up on the table.

HIT

After receiving one or more cards in this manner, when you are satisfied with your total, slide your two downcards under your chips in the betting space. If you have gone over a total of 21, turn your cards face up and place them in front of your betting space. The dealer will then collect your cards, along with your wager.

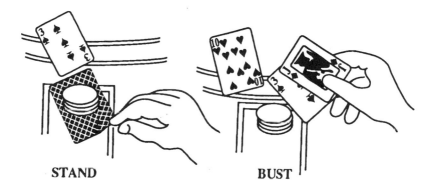

STAND   BUST

If you are permitted to double down and wish to exercise this option, turn both of your cards face up and place an additional wager of equal value next to your original wager. The dealer will then give you one more card, which is dealt face down.

DOUBLING DOWN

Should you wish to split a pair, turn both of your cards face up, separate them, and place an additional bet of equal value next to your original bet.

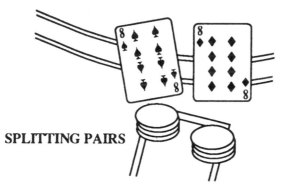

SPLITTING PAIRS

You now will have two hands and will play the one on your right to completion first. Blackjack etiquette dictates that you should not touch your cards after splitting. Consequently, to indicate that you want a "hit," scrape your hand or one of your fingers toward you on the felt. The dealer will then give you a card face up on the table. If you wish to stand pat, hold your hand palm down above your cards and wave it sideways. Once you are satisfied with your first hand, you will then play your second hand to completion in the same manner.

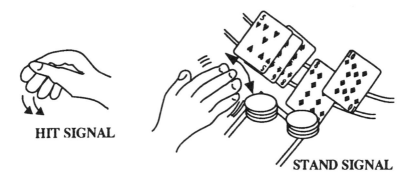

HIT SIGNAL

STAND SIGNAL

As mentioned earlier, when you split a pair of aces, the dealer will give you only one additional card, which is dealt face down, on each hand. Therefore, no signals are necessary.

SPLITTING ACES

In a blackjack game that is dealt face up, you should never touch your cards. The hand signals just described should be used to indicate whether you wish to hit or stand. When splitting or doubling down, place an additional bet in front of you on the table and verbally inform the dealer of what you wish to do.

It also should be noted here that as a courtesy to the dealer — and to protect yourself — you should not retrieve your winnings or place your next wager until the dealer has discarded all of your cards.

Finally, if you are not sure of the correct procedure, ask the dealer. It is his job not only to deal the cards and to collect and pay bets, but also to ensure that the game runs smoothly. Most dealers will be glad to give you any assistance you require.

Insurance

The insurance bet is one that requires special discussion. Suppose you are dealt a blackjack but the dealer has an ace up. If he also has a blackjack, you will push. Wouldn't it be nice to guarantee that you will win a bet?

Here's another example. Suppose you have a total of 20 and the dealer has an ace up. If you take insurance and the dealer has a blackjack, you will get your money back. If the dealer doesn't have a blackjack, there's a good chance that you will beat him and still show a profit.

So it seems as though insurance is a good deal. But let's discuss the insurance bet, analyze it mathematically, and then come to a conclusion about it.

Whenever the dealer has an ace up, you are allowed to wager an amount half the size of your original bet that the dealer's hole card has a value of 10. If the dealer does have a 10-value card, you win your insurance bet, which pays 2-to-1. But if the dealer does not have a 10-value card in the hole, you lose your insurance bet. When you win the insurance bet, no money changes hands (unless you have a blackjack), which makes it appear that this insurance was worth purchasing.

But let's take a closer look. Disregarding your cards for the moment, let's assume that you are playing in a single-deck game and that the dealer has an ace up. What are his chances of having a 10-value card in the hole? This is easy to calculate. Of the 51 cards remaining in the deck, 16 will have a value of 10 and 35 will have other values. This means that the odds against your bet being successful are 35-to-16 or 2.1875-to-1. The house advantage on this bet is almost 6 percent, since you are getting only a 2-to-1 payback on a 2.1875-to-1 shot.

If both of your cards are 10-value cards, the situation is even worse. Out of the remaining 49 cards in the deck (remember, we have removed the dealer's ace, plus your two cards), there will be only 14 cards with a value of 10. Now you will be getting 2-to-1 on a 2.5-to-1 proposition.

This brings us to our conclusion: Don't make the insurance bet. Even though it might seem like a good deal, it is very costly in the long run. (There is an exception to this, which is discussed in the "Card Counting" section of the text.)

Rule Variations and Other Options

Although the basics of "21" are standard, the games will differ slightly from casino to casino, depending on the rules in effect and the number of decks used, as well as on certain other options that may be available. Many rule variations and other options increase the house edge. But other rules and options are favorable for you, and you should be more inclined to play in casinos that offer these small advantages.

As a standard by which to judge variations and options, we will use the blackjack rules in effect at most Las Vegas Strip casinos, which are as follows:

● Players are permitted to double down on any first two cards.

● Any pair may be split.

- The dealer must stand on soft 17. A soft 17 is a hand composed of an ace, plus one or more cards that have a total count of 6. For example,

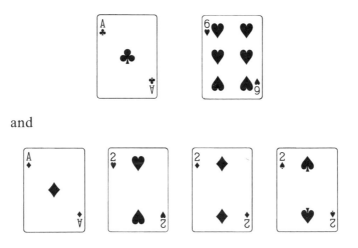

and

are both soft 17.

In a single-deck blackjack game with Las Vegas Strip rules, a player who uses perfect basic strategy will be playing virtually dead even with the house. However, the advantage will swing in either your favor or the casino's favor if any of the following options and rule variations are implemented:

1. More than one deck of cards is used. The more decks of cards in play, the larger the house advantage. One reason for this is that it's more difficult to make a blackjack in a multiple-deck game than it is in a single-deck game.

Regardless of whether you are playing in a single- or a multiple-deck game, the probability of the first card dealt being an ace is 1 ÷ 13 or 7.69 percent, and the probability of the first card having a value of 10 (ten, jack, queen, or king) is 4 ÷ 13 or 30.77 percent. But the probability of the first two cards being either an ace and a 10-value card or a 10-value card and an ace is correlated to the number of decks in use.

In a single-deck game, there are 1,326 two-card combinations, out of which 64 or 4.83 percent produce a blackjack. In a double-deck game, there are 5,356 two-card combinations, out of which 256 or 4.78 percent produce a blackjack. As you can see, you would prefer to play in a single-deck game than in a double-deck game.

Using two decks of cards, as compared to only one deck of cards, will increase the house advantage by 0.35 percent. Four decks in play will increase the house advantage by 0.51 percent, and six decks will increase the casino's edge by 0.60 percent.

2. The dealer must hit soft 17. When the dealer must hit a soft 17, the house advantage is increased by 0.20 percent. This rule is common in downtown Las Vegas and in most casinos in Northern Nevada. It is also widespread in most gambling venues outside of Nevada.

3. Players may double down on a total of 10 or 11 only. Being able to double down on any first two cards is one of the main advantages you have. When the house allows you to double down only on a total of 10 or 11, its advantage is increased by 0.28 percent.

4. Players may double down on a total of 11 only. This increases the house advantage by 0.69 percent.

5. Soft doubling is not allowed. If you cannot double down those times when your hand contains an ace, the house gains an advantage of 0.11 percent.

6. Players are not permitted to resplit pairs. This rule is not as severe as those just mentioned, but it still will cost the basic strategy player 0.02 percent.

7. Players are permitted to resplit aces. Normally, even in those casinos that otherwise allow resplitting of pairs, you cannot resplit aces. However, a few casinos do allow aces to be split more than once. This favorable rule is worth 0.06 percent to the basic strategy player.

8. Late surrender is offered. This favorable option allows you to turn in your first two cards in exchange for half of your original bet, as long as the dealer does not have a blackjack. Surrender is not available in very many casinos, but for the basic strategy player who makes correct use of this option, it is worth 0.02 percent in single-deck games and 0.07 percent in multiple-deck games.

9. Early surrender is offered. This rule allows you to surrender your hand before the dealer has checked for a natural. This makes a big difference and is worth 0.63 percent to the basic strategy player. When Atlantic City first legalized gambling, early surrender was part of its blackjack game. However, this great rule was removed in 1981 and is rarely seen today.

10. Players may double down after splitting. Some casinos will allow you to split a pair, draw a card, and then double down. Those few places that offer this favorable option give up 0.14 percent.

11. Drawing more than one card after splitting aces is permitted. A small number of casinos will allow you to draw more than one card on split aces. However, this option is worth only 0.03 percent to the basic strategy player.

12. Players may double down on more than two cards. A few casinos — mainly in Nevada — offer this favorable rule. When it is in effect, this option is worth 0.24 percent to the basic strategy player. (One casino in Las Vegas used to offer and advertise this option, but that casino also dealt a six-deck game.)

13. The blackjack payoff is 2-for-1. This absolutely great option is worth more than 2 percent to the basic strategy player. One casino in downtown Las Vegas has been known to offer "2-for-1 blackjack" (with no publicity) the week before Christmas for bets no larger than $5. (Unfortunately, that casino hasn't done it the last couple of years.) This bonus is also occasionally used as a promotion to attract business. Should you see it offered, take advantage of it.

14. The blackjack payoff is 2-for-1 if both your cards are red. Since red blackjacks will happen one-fourth of the time, this favorable rule is worth a little more than 0.5 percent to the basic strategy player.

15. The blackjack payoff is 6-to-5 in single-deck games with other favorable rules. This rule is usually offered in conjunction with other favorable rules, plus a single-deck game. However, the gain from the other rules (and the single deck) does not offset the loss of more than 1 percent that this payoff change produces.

16. Novelty bonuses are offered. These special options include a 2-for-1 payoff when you are dealt certain winning hands, such as three sevens or a hand like

In general, novelty bonuses are worthless. Nevertheless, you should be on the lookout for them, as a casino occasionally will make a miscalculation and its bonus option will be quite valuable.

17. Lose all to a natural is in effect. In most casinos, if you split or double down and it turns out that the dealer has a blackjack, you lose only your original bet. However, in some casinos outside the United States, you lose your additional bets as well. If lose all to a natural is in effect, the house advantage is increased by 0.11 percent.

18. Six-card automatic winner is offered. At the time of this writing, one casino in Nevada offers this option. It is worth 0.16 percent to the player, but does require some changes to correct basic strategy.

Basic Strategy

Getting Started Quickly

Basic strategy for "21" is not difficult to learn, but it does take some time to master. Because of this, we are providing a simplified version that will enable you to begin playing the game immediately. Although you won't attain the same level of success that the true basic strategist enjoys, you will do much better than the typical player if you adhere to the few rules that follow:

Rule No. 1: Hit a total of 12 if the dealer has a deuce or a trey up. Many players think that if the dealer has a bust card, they should stand pat on any total of 12 or higher. They are right about the "or higher" part, but if the dealer has a deuce or a trey up, you should hit a total of 12.

Rule No. 2: If the dealer has a four, five, or six up, stand on a total of 12 or higher. It is now correct to give the dealer every opportunity to bust. Playing a lucky hunch and taking a hit in these situations can prove very costly.

Rule No. 3: When the dealer has a seven, an eight, a nine, a 10-value card, or an ace up, hit your "hard" hands until you reach a total of 17. A "hard" hand is a hand that can have only one total count, as opposed to a "soft" hand, which contains an ace and therefore can be totaled in two ways. Although you often will bust when you hit a hard total of 15 or 16, you will lose less money in the long run by hitting these hands than by standing pat when the dealer has a high card up.

Rule No. 4: If you have a "soft" hand, always hit until you reach a total of 18. As just noted, a "soft" hand contains an ace, which can be counted as either 1 or 11. If you count your ace as 11, hit your soft total, and go over 21, you can then count your ace as 1 and follow the standard rules just given for hitting hard totals. For example, suppose you have

giving you a soft total of 14. If you catch a nine, you will have a hard total of 13 and should play your hand according to the standard rules for hard totals.

Rule No. 5: Always split aces and eights. Although you always should split these hands, the reason for splitting each pair is different. A pair of aces should be split because two 11-count hands are much more profitable than one hand that totals a count of 2 — even though you will receive only one additional card on each of your aces. In contrast, a pair of eights should be split because two 8-count hands are less unprofitable than one hand that totals 16. While playing a total of 8 versus a dealer's 10-value upcard is usually not profitable, playing a total of 16 against that same 10-value card is extremely unprofitable. Consequently, it is worth it in the long run to put an extra bet on the table, even though you occasionally might lose twice as much money.

Rule No. 6: Never split a pair of fours, fives, or tens. When we refer to a pair of tens, we are including hands like

The reason for never splitting a pair of 10-value cards should be obvious: A total of 20 is too good to give up. So is a total of 10, and the same is true for a total of 8 when the alternative is two 4-count starting hands.

Rule No. 7: Split a pair of deuces, treys, sixes, sevens, and nines when the dealer has a four, five, or six up. The reason for splitting these pairs is that a four, a five, or a six upcard is a premier bust card for the dealer. If you are unlucky and fail to make quality totals on your hands, the dealer still will have a good chance of going over 21. Thus you would like to put more money on the table.

Rule No. 8: Always double down when you have a total of 11, unless the dealer has an ace up. A total of 11 is a very strong starting hand. It is superior to any dealer upcard, except an ace, which is also worth 11. In other words, you should take advantage of this profitable opportunity and double your bet.

Rule No. 9: Always double down when you have a total of 10, unless the dealer has either an ace or a 10-value card up. The reasoning here is identical to that given for Rule No. 8. Since you have a big advantage with a total of 10 versus a dealer upcard of a deuce through a nine, you should put more money on the table.

Rule No. 10: Double down on soft totals of 13 through 18 when the dealer has a five or a six up. When you double down on soft totals in these situations, you won't make a quality hand most of the time, but the dealer often will go over 21. Occasionally, however, the dealer won't bust, but you will catch a perfect card that enables you to win anyway. It is the combination of these two circumstances that makes soft doubling profitable.

Nevertheless, soft doubling does not add much to your expectation. So if you wish to ignore this rule, you can do so with little penalty.

Rule No. 11: Never take insurance. As noted earlier, this bet should not be made, as it is very costly in the long run. The one exception to this rule is discussed in the "Card Counting" section of the booklet.

Basic Strategy

There is only one correct decision for any given situation in blackjack, and that decision is based strictly on mathematics. Developed by computer analysis, these correct decisions as a whole are referred to as basic strategy, which dictates the optimum way to play your hand versus the dealer's upcard. In other words, only your two cards and the dealer's upcard are considered. Cards in other players' hands are ignored, as are those cards you may have seen in a previous round of play.

As we noted in the previous section, once you have mastered basic strategy and can apply it correctly, you will be playing almost dead even with any casino that offers a single-deck game and Las Vegas Strip rules.

Although basic strategy will vary slightly depending on the number of decks used and the exact rules in effect, the differences will have only a small effect on your expectation. Consequently, the basic strategy that follows can be used for virtually every game of blackjack that you will ever play, and you need not be concerned with the slight variations between it and "perfect" basic strategy.

A word of caution: Many people believe they play a "good" basic strategy, but in reality they don't play much better than the typical tourist. Part of the reason for this is that most basic strategy plays are the same as those that an intuitive player would make. But there are enough differences that you need to take the time to learn exactly what is correct.

The first decision that you should make after receiving your cards is whether to split. You, of course, will have the option of splitting only if you are dealt two cards of the same rank. The correct pair-splitting strategies are given in Table I.

Table I: Pair Splitting

Pair	Split if Dealer's Upcard Is
Aces	Any Card
Tens	Never Split
Nines	Deuce – Six, Eight, Nine
Eights	Any Card
Sevens	Deuce – Seven
Sixes	Trey – Six
Fives	Never Split
Fours	Never Split
Treys	Four – Seven
Deuces	Four – Seven

If you do not have the option of splitting, you should next consider whether to double down. Even though we are assuming that you are permitted to double down on any first two cards, you will not exercise this option on most of your hands. The correct double-down strategies for hard and soft totals are shown in Table II and Table III.

Table II: Hard Doubling

Starting Total	Double if Dealer's Upcard Is
11	Deuce – Ten
10	Deuce – Nine
9	Trey – Six

Table III: Soft Doubling

Starting Hand	Double if Dealer's Upcard Is
A7	Trey – Six
A6	Trey – Six
A5	Four – Six
A4	Four – Six
A3	Five, Six
A2	Five, Six

Doubling down on soft totals is not as profitable as it is on hard totals. Nevertheless, it is still correct to double down on the soft hands listed versus the appropriate dealer upcard, so don't neglect this play.

If you do not exercise the option to double down, you must decide either to hit or to stand. But prior to making this decision, you must take into account whether you have a soft hand. When you do, you should follow the strategy provided in Table IV.

Table IV: Hitting Soft Hands

Dealer's Upcard	Hit if Your Total Is
Nine, Ten, or Ace	Less than Soft 19
All Others	Less than Soft 18

If you do not exercise the option to double down and you hold a hard hand, you should follow the strategy given in Table V.

Table V: Hitting Hard Hands

Dealer's Upcard	Hit if Your Total Is
Deuce or Trey	Less than 13
Four, Five, or Six	Less than 12
Seven, Eight, Nine, Ten, or Ace	Less than 17

Although all of the strategy tables are important, Table V is the most important. Fortunately, it is also the easiest to remember.

Surrender

As noted in the section titled "Rule Variations and Other Options," the surrender option permits you to turn in your first two cards in exchange for half of your bet.

However, as already mentioned, there are actually two types of surrender. The first is referred to as "early surrender," which allows you to give up your hand before the dealer looks at his hole card. This is a terrific option that reduces a casino's advantage by more than 0.6 percent for the basic strategy player. In fact, in most games, this option will give the basic strategy player an edge over the house.

When gambling first became legal in Atlantic City, early surrender was standard in all East Coast casinos. And though Atlantic City offered only six-deck games, these were some of the best games in the world. Unfortunately, this is not the case anymore, and we know of no casino in the United States that currently offers early surrender, though it does appear on rare occasions.

The second type of surrender is known as "late surrender," which permits you to relinquish your first two cards only after the dealer has checked his hole card to determine that he does not have a blackjack. Late surrender is still offered in a few casinos. If you are playing where this option is available, you should first make the decision on splitting pairs if appropriate, then determine whether to surrender your hand, according to the strategy given in table VI.

Table VI: Surrender

Starting Total	Surrender if Dealer's Upcard Is
16 (not 8,8)	Nine, Ten, or Ace
15	Ten

The reason for making the split decision prior to the surrender decision is because of one hand — a pair of eights, which always should be split. Never surrender this hand. However, if you are dealt any other two-card combination that totals 16 and the dealer has a nine, a 10-value card, or an ace up, surrender your hand if the casino offers this option.

Deviating From Basic Strategy

We want to pause for a moment and comment on what happens when you deviate from basic strategy. In the short run, you might do better and you might do worse. That's because there is much short term-luck in blackjack. This is why a terrible player will frequently leave the table a winner, and sometimes be a big winner.

But in the long run, if you occasionally play hunches or vary from basic strategy for other reasons, you can expect to have inferior results. That's why we emphasize the need to thoroughly learn basic strategy and to stick to it.

Basic Strategy Quiz

Although basic strategy is not difficult to learn, it does take time and study to master. To help you in this endeavor, we have prepared the following short quiz.

1. You have a total of 12, and the dealer has a trey up. Do you hit or stand?

Hit. Remember, just because the dealer has a bust card up does not mean that you automatically should stand with a total of more than 11. Always hit a total of 12 when the dealer has either a deuce or a trey up.

2. You started with ace-deuce, the dealer started with a seven up, and you hit and caught a five, giving you a soft 18. Do you hit or stand?

Stand on a soft 18 unless the dealer's upcard is a nine, a ten, or an ace. In these situations, you need at least a soft 19 to stand.

3. You have a total of 11 on your first two cards, and the dealer has an ace up. Do you double down?

No. With a total of 11, you should double down against any dealer upcard except an ace. When the dealer has an ace up, you should just hit.

4. You are dealt a pair of eights, which totals 16, and the dealer's upcard is an ace. Should you surrender?

No. Remember, you are supposed to consider the splitting option before you consider the surrender option. Always split a pair of eights.

5. You are dealt a nine and a seven, for a total of 16, and the dealer's upcard is a nine. What should you do?

> If you are playing in a casino that offers surrender, give up your hand. If surrender is not available, hit and hope you don't bust.

6. You are dealt a pair of fours, and the dealer has a three up. Do you split?

> No. Starting with one hand that has a total of 8 is much better than starting with two hands that each total 4. A pair of fours should never be split.

7. What other pairs should never be split?

> A pair of fives and a pair of 10-value cards.

8. You have a blackjack, but the dealer has an ace up. Should you take insurance?

> No. Never take insurance, unless you have learned to accurately count cards.

9. You have a hard total of 15, and the dealer has an eight up. Do you hit or stand?

> Hit. If the dealer has a seven, an eight, a nine, a 10-value card, or an ace up, always hit your hard hands until you have at least a total of 17. Standing on a smaller total against one of these upcards occasionally will win when the dealer busts, but in the long run, this play will prove to be very expensive.

10. You have a pair of nines, and the dealer has a seven up. Should you split?

> No. You should stand. It is easy to see why this play is correct. If the dealer has a 10-value card in the hole — which is his most likely holding — your total of 18 will beat his total of 17.

11. You have a two-card total of 9, and the dealer has a seven up. Do you double down?

No. You need a starting total of 10 or 11 to make this play. Double down with a total of 9 only when the dealer shows a trey, four, five, or six up.

12. Your first two cards are an ace and a trey, and the dealer has a five up. Should you double down?

Yes. When you start with a soft 13 through a soft 18, it is correct to double down when the dealer has a five or a six up.

13. You have a hard total of 8 on your first two cards, and the dealer has a four up. Do you double down?

No. Never double down with a hard total of less than 9. Also, never double down with a hard total of more than 11.

14. Suppose you split two sevens when the dealer has a five up, and you catch another seven. What should you do?

Split again if the rules allow you to do so.

15. Suppose the dealer has a 10-value card up, and you start with a hard total of 15 and catch an ace, giving you a hard total of 16. Should you hit again?

Absolutely. Remember, you are supposed to hit a hard hand until you reach a total of 17 when the dealer has a seven, an eight, a nine, a 10-value card, or an ace up. The fact that you already have hit once does not change your decision.

16. Suppose your starting total is 11, and you double down and catch a deuce. Did you play your hand wrong?

No. Remember, the correct basic strategy play is the most advantageous play in the long run. Just because you lose a hand does not mean that you played it wrong. Moreover, in the situation just described, the dealer may still bust.

17. Suppose you start with an ace and a seven, and the dealer has a 10-value card up. Do you hit or stand?

You must hit. Standing on a soft 18 in this spot is a very common and costly mistake that inexperienced players make.

18. Suppose you start with a total of 15, and the dealer has an eight up. Should you surrender?

No. Even though you don't particularly like your hand, giving up half a bet is too large a price to pay in this situation.

19. You have a soft total of 12, and the dealer has a five up. Do you stand?

No. Since you have a soft 12, you must have two aces, which always should be split. If you had a hard 12, then you would stand.

20. How often should you review basic strategy?

The answer depends on how much you value your money. If you are a novice player, we suggest that you review the basic strategy tables prior to each time you play. Once you have gained some experience, a periodic review should be sufficient.

Card Counting

Introduction

Suppose that you are playing blackjack heads up with the dealer, and there are only four cards left in the deck or shoe. Further suppose that you know these four cards are composed of three 10-value cards and an ace. What will happen?

First, notice that half the time you will be dealt two 10-value cards and the dealer will be dealt a blackjack. When this is the case, you will lose your bet. But also notice that half the time you will be dealt the blackjack and the dealer will receive the two 10-value cards. When this occurs, you automatically will win one and one-half bets.

As you can see, you expect to lose one bet half of the time, but the other half of the time, you expect to gain one and one-half bets. This is the same as averaging a profit of one-fourth bet every time you play a hand under the circumstances just described. Wouldn't it be great if you always knew the composition of the cards remaining to be dealt?

This is the type of information you can obtain from what is known as counting cards. Unfortunately, your information won't be quite this precise. But you will know when more high cards than low cards remain in the deck, and vice versa.

High cards are favorable for you, while low cards are beneficial to the house. This should seem intuitively correct to you after you have played blackjack for only a short period of time. A lot of high cards remaining in the deck means more blackjacks and more good starting hands. In contrast, a lot of small cards yet to be dealt means more hands with values from 12 through 16 — known as stiff hands. Moreover, with many small cards remaining, it is less likely the dealer will bust when he is forced to hit a hand that has a total of less than 17.

There are many different card counting systems, but they all are premised on the same ideas. Some systems are extremely complicated. Others, however, are relatively simple and easy to learn, yet they still provide an effective means of identifying many of those situations where you actually will have the best of it in a "21" game.

Incidentally, many blackjack players find card counting to be an enjoyable undertaking. It adds a new dimension to the way you play the game, plus being able to play when you and the house essentially have changed places is a rewarding endeavor.

Card Counting Myths

Numerous myths surround the subject of card counting and serve to dissuade many players from even attempting to learn this skill. So before we discuss one of the simple card counting systems and how to use it, we'd like to dispel some of the more common fictitious notions associated with counting down a deck or a shoe.

Myth No. 1: You must memorize every card. In reality, as you will soon see, all that's necessary when counting cards is to add and subtract. If total card memorization was required, virtually no one would be able to do it. In fact, if card counting meant remembering every card, it's doubtful that anyone ever would have made the effort to master this skill.

Myth No. 2: Card counters routinely win huge sums of money from the casinos. Card counting does work. By carefully selecting the games you play in and by being very disciplined, you can gain a small edge over the house. But few people are actually able to make a living at playing blackjack. To be this successful, you need to be highly proficient at card counting, and you also must have a good act. That is, you must convince casino personnel that you are not someone they need to take seriously.

Myth No. 3: Card counting will enable you to beat all blackjack games. Card counting will permit you to beat only those games in which a significant number of cards is dealt from the deck or shoe. In theory, you could beat virtually any blackjack game by making large enough bets when your counting system has identified that you have the best of it. But realistically, exceptionally large bets should not be made for two reasons. First, you will place your gambling bankroll in jeopardy, and second, you immediately will alert casino personnel that they need to observe your action very closely. If the casino identifies you as a card counter, you may discover that your game has become much more difficult to beat. The house might shuffle up sooner than it normally would, restrict how much you are allowed to vary your bet, and sometimes even ask you to take your action elsewhere.

Myth No. 4: You need to make huge bets to get an edge over the house. The key to card counting is to select good games. The attributes that you should be looking for are favorable rules and deep deck penetration. When you have found such a game, you can gain an overall advantage with only a reasonable bet variation. That is, you bet more when your count has identified that you have the edge. If a huge bet variation is required to gain the advantage, that particular game is probably not worth playing.

Myth No. 5: If you miss a card, your count becomes worthless. When counting cards, you of course want to see as many cards as possible. But if you miss a card every now and then, it is no big deal. Simply pretend that the card you missed is still in the deck, and continue with your count as though nothing has happened.

Myth No. 6: Card counters win every time they play. In blackjack, as in all gambling games, there is a great deal of short-term luck. Put another way, you can play poorly and do quite well for a short period of time. You also can play skillfully and do badly for a short period of time. Unfortunately, these short periods of time sometimes can last longer than you might think is possible. The moral of this is that even the most highly skilled players will have lots of losing sessions, lots of losing days, and even occasional losing trips to their favorite gambling center. Skilled card counters do not come close to winning every time they play. But in the long run, they expect to be ahead.

Myth No. 7: When the count is favorable (unfavorable), you will get more good (bad) hands than the dealer. A favorable count tells you that the balance of the deck or shoe is "rich" in high cards and aces. Suppose you know that an excess of 10-value cards is remaining in the undealt portion of the deck. Does this mean that you are more likely than the dealer is to be dealt two 10-value cards, for a total of 20? Of course not. The dealer has the same probability of being dealt a good hand as you do.

A favorable count indicates two things. First, you will be dealt more blackjacks than normal, which pay 3-to-2. Second, you will be dealt fewer stiff hands than normal, meaning that you will bust less often. Remember, one advantage that the house has over the player is that the player must act first. If both you and the dealer go over 21, you still lose. But when you receive fewer stiff hands, this particular casino advantage is reduced.

The High-Low Count

Prior to discussing the High-Low Count system, we'd like to remind you that high cards are to your advantage while low cards favor the house. Card counting will help you identify those times when the deck is rich in high cards. It is as simple as adding and subtracting the number 1, and you should be able to learn the basics of counting cards in a short period of time.

The High-Low Count is very simple, yet it is almost as powerful as any other counting system available, no matter how complex that other system may be.

At the beginning of a fresh deck or shoe, after the dealer has shuffled, you start with a count of 0. Each time you see an ace, a king, a queen, a jack, or a ten, subtract 1 from your count; each time you see a deuce, trey, four, five, or six, add 1 to your count. And when you see a seven, an eight, or a nine, ignore them as far as the count is concerned. (In other words, add 0 to your count.) Let's look at a few examples.

Example No. 1: If the first three cards you see are

your count is -1.

Example No. 2: If the first three cards you see are

your count is 0.

Example No. 3: If the first five cards you see are

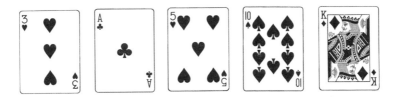

your count is -1.

Example No. 4: If the first six cards you see are

your count is +3.

Example No. 5: If the first seven cards you see are

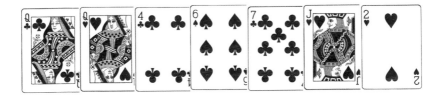

your count is 0.

Notice that we said to count the "cards that you see." Remember, if you have missed a card, just ignore it. Also, whenever the dealer shuffles, you should restart your count at 0.

Finally, you will need to do considerable practicing on your own before you try to count cards in a casino. You should be able to count down a deck in less than 60 seconds. We suggest that you start by turning over and counting one card at a time. Once you become proficient at this, turn over two cards simultaneously and count them, then turn over three cards at a time and count them. If your count does not end in 0 after you complete the deck, you have made an error.

We want to emphasize how important this practice is. Even though the idea behind card counting is very simple, and the technique just presented is also simple, implementing it in a casino environment won't come automatically. A typical person needs as much as 20 hours of practice on his "kitchen table" before he is ready for the casino.

Using the Count

To keep this discussion simple, we're going to assume that you're playing in a single-deck game. This means that we will be concerned only with what is referred to as the "running count." If you are playing in a multideck game, it will be necessary to convert the running count into the "true count," which is discussed in the next section of this booklet.

The running count can be defined as your count — the tally of all cards put into play that you see. For example, if you have a cumulative count of +2 after seeing seven cards, the running count is +2. This figure, the running count, determines two things:

1. How much you should bet, and

2. Whether you should play your hand differently from the standard basic strategy.

Prior to playing, we suggest that you divide your gambling bankroll into at least 100 units and preferably 200 or more units. We personally prefer and recommend 400 units, as this will allow you to withstand more negative fluctuations without going broke.

But if you are more adventurous than we are, you may want to play with only 100 units or some number in between.

Betting should proceed as follows: If the running count is +1 or less (less means either 0 or a negative number), bet only one unit; if the running count is +2, +3, or +4, bet two units; if the running count is greater than +4, bet either three or four units. Your decision — whether to bet three or four units — should be based on how venturesome you are and on how much bet variation you think a particular casino will tolerate.

Let's look at a specific example. Suppose your gambling bankroll is $1,000 and you divide it into 200 units. This means that your basic bet is $5. If the running count is -3, bet $5; if your count is -1, bet $5; if the count is 0, bet $5. If the running count is +2, bet $10, and if the count is +6, bet either $15 or $20.

As noted, the running count also determines when you should play differently from what basic strategy dictates. There are more than 100 deviations from basic strategy that can be made, but only a few of them are really important. The ones we recommend are as follows:

- When the running count is +1 or higher, stand on a total of 16 when the dealer has a 10-value card up.

- If the running count is +4 or higher, stand on a total of 15 when the dealer has a 10-value card up.

- If the running count is -1 or less, hit a total of 12 when the dealer has a four up.

One additional play you should consider is whether to take insurance, and this is the most important decision you will make. As you will recall, we stated earlier that since insurance pays 2-to-1 and the odds of the dealer having a 10-value card beneath an ace are higher than that, you should not make this bet. However, the running count will identify those times when many high cards remain in the undealt portion of the deck. Consequently, when playing in a single-deck game, you should take insurance whenever the running count is +2 or higher.

Playing in Multideck Games

If you are playing in a single-deck blackjack game and the first six cards you see are low cards, giving you a count of +6, this means that there are six more high cards remaining in the deck than there are low cards. This enormous difference provides you with a significant advantage over the house.

But suppose you are playing against a six-deck shoe and the first six cards you see are low cards. Again, this means that there are six more high cards than there are low cards remaining in the shoe. But is your advantage very large?

The answer is no. In fact, you are still at a disadvantage, as you are averaging only one extra high card per deck and you have not overcome the extra disadvantage of playing against a multiple-deck shoe.

To handle this problem, you must convert your running count into what is referred to as the "true count." This is simply the running count divided by the number of decks that remain in the shoe. As examples, if the running count is +8 and there are four decks remaining, the true count is +2; if the running count is -6 and two decks remain, the true count is -3; and if the running count is +2 and there is only one-half deck remaining, the true count is +4.

For placing correct bets in a shoe game, your true count must be one higher than the appropriate running count for a single-deck game. Specifically, you should bet as follows:

● If the true count is +2 or less, bet only one unit.

- If the true count is +3, +4, or +5, bet two units.

- If the true count is greater than +5, bet either three or four units. Sometimes when playing against a shoe, you may want to bet even more if the true count is higher than +5.

You should always use this true-count betting strategy when you are playing in a multiple-deck game, even if there is only one deck remaining in the shoe. The single-deck indices given in the previous section of this booklet should be used only when you are playing in a single-deck game.

However, for the three strategy changes provided in the previous section, you should use the true count in a multideck game that corresponds with the running count given for a single-deck game. In other words, if the true count is +1 or higher, stand on a total of 16 when the dealer has a 10-value card up. If the true count is +4 or higher, stand on a total of 15 when the dealer has a 10-value card up, and if the true count is -1 or less, hit a total of 12 when the dealer has a four up.

You also should take insurance when the count becomes high enough. However, when playing in a multiple-deck game, you require a true count of +3 before exercising this option.

More advanced concepts on card counting can be found in the books listed in the "Recommended Reading" section.

Card Counting Tips

As you have just seen, counting cards is not as difficult as it appears to be. But here are a few tips that will make this endeavor even easier.

Tip No. 1: Learn to cancel counts. When a card that has a count of +1 appears with a card that has a count of -1, together they have a count of 0. You should be able to recognize these combinations and count them as one entity. (That is, you can ignore them.) Canceling counts is one of the secrets of successful card counting and is why some experts can count down a deck extremely quickly. It takes practice to pick up this skill, but once mastered, canceling counts greatly facilitates card counting.

Tip No. 2: Try to play heads up with the dealer. If no other players are at the table, you can play more hands. The more hands you play, the more money you can put in action, and the more money you put in action, the higher your expectation should be. Remember, even with correct counting, your edge is still quite small, so you need to play as many hands as possible for your advantage to become meaningful.

Tip No. 3: Share your cards with other players. The more information you have at the blackjack table, the better your play will be. One way of gaining information is to share your hand with the other players at your table, especially those sitting on your left who will act after you. Once this friendship has begun, you usually can expect these players to reciprocate and show you their hands.

Tip No. 4: Don't sit down in the middle of a shoe. Unless specific knowledge of the card distribution in a shoe is known, all blackjack players, no matter how skilled they may be, are at a disadvantage. Consequently, when entering a shoe game, you want to start at the beginning of a shoe, because the composition of the cards changes slowly.

Tip No. 5: Don't enter a single-deck game if big cards appeared on the previous round and there was no shuffle. In a single-deck game, if a lot of high cards were dealt on the previous round, unless the dealer shuffles, the rest of the deck will be significantly rich in small cards, meaning that one's expectation is negative. Therefore, it is best to wait for a new shuffle before sitting down.

Card Counting Quiz

We have covered a great deal of material in this section on card counting. To see whether you have absorbed it all, we have prepared another short quiz for you. Good luck.

1. If the first five cards you see are

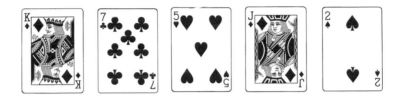

   What is your count?
   Your count is 0.

2. If the true count is +4, how much should you bet?
   You should wager two betting units.

3. What type of games will card counting enable you to beat?
   Card counting will enable you to beat only those games where a significant number of cards are dealt from the deck or shoe.

4. What is the running count?
   The running count is your count, the cumulative total of all cards you have seen.

5. What is meant by canceling counts?
   To cancel counts means that if a card having a value of +1 appears with a card having a value of -1, you count them together as 0.

6. Suppose you have a total of 12, the dealer has a four up, and the true count is -3. What should you do?
  Hit.

7. What cards receive a positive count, what cards receive a negative count, and what cards receive a count of 0?
  Aces, kings, queens, jacks, and tens receive a count of -1; deuces, treys, fours, fives, and sixes receive a count of +1; sevens, eights, and nines receive a count of 0.

8. Why should you try to play heads up?
  Because you will be able to play more hands.

9. What is the true count?
  The true count is the running count divided by the number of decks that remain in a shoe.

10. In a single-deck game, if the running count is +3, should you stand on a total of 15 when the dealer shows a 10-value card?
  No. You need a running count of +4 for this play to be correct. However, you should stand on a total of 16 against a dealer's ten with a count of +3.

11. When the count is positive, is it true that you will be dealt more good hands than the dealer?
  No. You won't be dealt more good hands than the dealer. However, you will be dealt more blackjacks than normal, and the dealer will bust more when he draws to stiff hands.

12. Why is it wrong to sit down in the middle of a shoe?
  Unless specific knowledge of the card distribution in a shoe is known, all blackjack players, no matter how skilled they may be, are at a disadvantage.

13. How many betting units should your gambling bankroll consist of?

   We suggest that you divide your gambling bankroll into at least 100 units and preferably 200 or more units. We personally prefer 400 units.

14. If the first seven cards you see are

What is the count?

   The count is -1.

15. What does card counting accomplish?

   It helps you to identify those times when the deck is rich in high cards.

16. What should you do if you miss a card when counting?

   Just ignore it.

17. Why should you not make exceptionally large bets?

   There are two reasons. First, you will put your gambling bankroll in jeopardy, and second, you will alert the house that it needs to observe your action very closely.

18. To take insurance in a multideck game, how high should your true count be?

   It must be +3 or higher.

19. Before attempting to count cards in a casino, how fast should you be able to count down a deck?

    You should be able to count down a deck in 60 seconds.

20. Does card counting guarantee that you will always win?

    Not at all. Remember, there is a lot of luck in blackjack, and you often will have a losing session, even when the game is good.

Other Topics

We're almost done. But there are four additional topics worth addressing that can significantly affect your play: money management, betting systems, casino comps, and what are referred to as "unbalanced counts."

Money Management Fallacies

Money management is a subject that seems to find its way into the majority of books written on gambling, so it might as well be addressed here. Though many gaming authors claim that the real secret to gambling success is proper management of your bankroll, little of what has been written is accurate.

We covered this topic to some extent when we discussed dividing your bankroll into betting units and how much you should bet according to the count. This information is all you need to know about money management to be successful at "21." Nevertheless, let's examine a few of the fallacies that constantly crop up concerning this subject.

(By the way, proper handling of your gambling bankroll is critical, and expert gamblers often refer to this as "bankroll management." This is very different from what many authors call money management.)

Fallacy No. 1: A formula exists that tells you when you have won enough money to quit playing. For most gambling games, formulas *do* exist that tell you how much you can expect to win or lose and what kind of fluctuations to anticipate. But no formula exists that tells you when you have won enough money to cash out. Our advice is this: If you think you are in a good game and want to continue playing, then do so. Otherwise, quit.

Fallacy No. 2: A formula exists that tells you when you have lost enough money to quit playing. The idea of a stop-loss does not mathematically exist. Once you have lost some money, there are many reasons to stop playing. As an example, perhaps you've become tired and are making too many mistakes. But there is no stop-loss formula that will let you know when it is time to quit playing. Though you must remember that there is a great deal of short-term luck in blackjack, if your game is good and your skills are sharp, it makes sense to keep playing.

Fallacy No. 3: Never risk your entire bankroll in one session. Suppose you make a $10 bet. Does it matter whether you have $200 or $2,000 on the table? Of course not. On the other hand, splitting your bankroll into several smaller "session" bankrolls is not incorrect. We consider this a personal matter, and you should do what makes you feel the most comfortable.

Fallacy No. 4: You need some minimum amount of money to play a particular game. The larger your basic betting unit is in relation to your bankroll, the more money you can expect to make, but the more likely you are to go broke. In addition, the larger your bankroll is, the higher the stakes you can play and still maintain an acceptable risk of going broke.

However, we tend to be conservative. That's why we advise that you split your bankroll into 400 units. But should you choose to divide your bankroll into a smaller number of units, you are not playing poorly, as we believe the amount of risk that you are willing to take is a personal decision.

Some Thoughts on Systems

Card counting, as we have discussed it, is actually a system. But, in general, most systems we see recommended in the gambling literature are not worth much, as they are related only to how you bet and your previous results. Nothing else is taken into consideration.

What makes card counting unique is that it identifies those times when you, not the casino, have the best of it. In contrast, betting systems usually recommend that you bet more when losing in an effort to recover your losses. This presents a serious problem: If you have a prolonged losing streak — and the laws of probability state that if you play blackjack long enough, you eventually will get unlucky and have a prolonged losing streak — you will get wiped out.

Another author put it this way: "If someone says he has a great system, tell him he can't borrow any money six months from now." We agree completely.

In the past few years, a new type of system has appeared in some of the blackjack literature. It is based on the idea that biases can be introduced in the deck, since a human shuffle is not always a "random" shuffle. The theory is that decks (or shoes) can develop where the dealer breaks too much and other good things begin to happen, such as drawing a 10-value card much more often than you should when doubling down.

The fact is, there is a tremendous amount of short-term luck in blackjack. This means that in a large casino containing many tables, there is bound to be a table where the dealer, in some recent period of time, has gone over 21 more than what normally would be expected, or where some of the players have caught all the cards they need. However, there is no reason to believe this pseudo trend will continue.

If at some time in the future you are tempted to purchase one of these systems — and they usually are very expensive — our advice is to save your money. Stick to proven techniques, such as basic strategy and card counting, that actually work.

Casino Comps

Casinos expect to win, and most of their customers expect the casinos to win. Of course, both parties know that on any given night the outcome can be different, but in general the money goes to the house. If this weren't the case, there wouldn't be so many casinos, and they wouldn't be built as lavishly as most of them are.

To help compensate for their advantage, and to make your gambling experience more enjoyable and thus encourage you to come back for another visit and another turn at the gambling tables, virtually all casinos offer comps to their better customers. These comps can include food — which can range from a small discount at a snack bar to a fabulous gourmet meal in a terrific restaurant — free rooms, free shows with great seats, transportation refunds, special parties for invited guests, and passes to other casino attractions.

Generally, casinos figure that the typical player will lose approximately 1.5 percent to 2 percent of total betting action, and they are willing to return a portion of this to ensure that their customers' gambling experience is as enjoyable as possible. Sometimes as much as 30 to 40 percent of your expected loss can be redeemed in this way.

Now, that 1.5 percent to 2 percent may not seem like much, but in time it can add up, especially in a fast-paced game like blackjack. So the casino can afford to treat you well.

But notice that when playing blackjack, if you master the techniques described in this book, you should be playing close to break even, and may at times even have a small advantage over the casino. Now add in a few comps, and you are actually a legitimate winner.

Usually, what will happen when you begin a blackjack session, unless you are playing for very small stakes, is that the supervisor in the blackjack pit will ask if you would like to be rated. If you answer in the affirmative, the supervisor will watch and track your play and estimate your average bet size. That, plus the length of time that you play, will determine what comps you may be eligible for.

Some casinos may want to issue you a "playing card" that identifies you with a tracking number. If you are interested in receiving any comps, accept this card and present it every time you play in this particular casino. The casino will now have a record of your total action and can fully reward you for your play.

In addition, a host may introduce himself to you and present you with his personal business card. This will enable you to call him any time, and he can issue you a comp even when you are not in the casino. It will be there waiting for you to arrive.

Finally, we advise you not to be shy. When you are playing or just after you've concluded a session, the best way to receive a comp is to ask for one. It's true that on occasion a casino host might introduce himself and invite you to "dinner on the house," but usually you need to initiate the action.

Unbalanced Counts

The card counting system that we've presented in this book is an example of what is known as a "balanced count." For a count to be considered balanced you must start with a count of 0, and if all the cards in the deck (or shoe) were to be dealt out, you would finish with a count of 0.

But there is another approach to counting cards, which comes under the umbrella of what are known as "unbalanced counts." Typically in these unbalanced counts, more cards are assigned a positive integer (or point value) than a negative integer.

You start with what is referred to as an "initial running count" (dependent on the number of decks used) and then either increase or decrease this count, depending on the point value assigned to the card that is currently in play. For example, if your initial running count is -4 and the first card in play is a small card that has an assigned point value of +1, your new running count would be -3.

The counting is continued in this manner. But since the count is unbalanced, it will tend to increase. That is, if all the cards are dealt out, you won't finish with the initial running count as you would if you were using a balanced count. You will finish with a number *higher* than the one that you started with. Put another way, if you started with a count of 0 and dealt out all the cards in the deck (or shoe), you would finish with a count higher than 0.

Of course, counting at blackjack is all about determining when you have an advantage. In unbalanced counts, depending on the number of decks in play, if your running count meets or exceeds a specific number, you have the edge. This is known as the "key count."

For example, one popular unbalanced count is the "Knock-Out Count." If you were to use this count in a double-deck game, your initial running count would be -4 and your key count would be +1. That is, instead of starting your count at 0, you would start it at -4, and whenever the running count reached +1 (or higher), you would have the advantage and would want to bet more than one unit. If you were to use this count in an eight-deck game, your initial running count would be -28 and your key count would be -6.

This may all sound very confusing, and we won't discuss these counts in any more detail here. But notice that we never mentioned the necessity of using a true-count conversion to determine whether you have an advantage. This means that you don't have to estimate the number of decks not yet in play, nor do you have to perform the appropriate division function when at the blackjack table.

Because of this, some people believe that unbalanced counts are easier to use than the better known and more commonly utrilized balanced counts. In addition, unbalanced counts have been shown to perform well when compared to balanced counts.

For those of you interested in pursuing unbalanced counts some of the recommended reading includes discussions of them. If you don't like to do simple division and estimate the number of decks not yet in play, unbalanced counts might be a better approach than the simple counting system presented in this book.

Conclusion

In the *Fundamentals of "21,"* we have attempted to provide you with a sound strategy for playing the popular casino game of blackjack. Although there is no such thing as a guaranteed win — no matter how skilled a player you are — following the advice given in this booklet will enable you to be much more successful than the majority of newcomers to this game.

We suggest that prior to each blackjack session, you review basic strategy. This is the most crucial element of successful play, and without a good grasp of this information, you will have little chance of winning in the long run. In addition, be certain that you are proficient at counting cards before attempting this skill in a casino.

Finally, although a great deal of short-term luck is involved in "21," a knowledgeable player can obtain a small edge over the house. Because of this, casino blackjack not only is exciting and challenging, but can be financially rewarding as well.

Glossary

Action: The total amount you bet on all hands played.

Back count: To stand behind a table and count the cards, waiting for a positive true count before making a wager. Because of back counting, some casinos do not allow mid-shoe entry into their games.

Basic strategy: The correct way to play your hand, given your total and the dealer's upcard.

Betting spread: The range of bets that one makes. If you range your bets between one and five units, then you are said to use a betting spread of 1-to-5.

Blackjack: Two cards totaling 21, an ace and a 10-value card. A blackjack pays 3-to-2.

Burn card: The top card of a deck or shoe that is removed from play. Also, a card is usually **burned** when a new dealer takes over if the deck or shoe is not reshuffled.

Bust: To go over the total of 21.

Camouflage: The deliberate making of an error in your play in an attempt to convince the house that you are not counting cards.

Card counter: A player who uses a counting system to track the cards to determine when he has the best of it.

Check: Another name for a gaming token or chip.

Comp: A complimentary service, such as a free meal or show, given to a preferred customer.

Cut card: A solid-colored piece of plastic that is inserted into a deck or shoe to indicate when it is time to reshuffle.

Dealer: An employee of the casino who deals the cards, collects bets, pays winning hands, and so forth.

Discards: The cards used since the last shuffle. They are usually stacked at the side of the table.

Double down: An option that allows the player to double his bet after seeing the first two cards. Only one additional card may be received after doubling down on a hand.

Double after splitting: An option that allows the player to double his bet after receiving the second card on any card that was originally part of a split pair.

Double exposure: A form of blackjack in which both dealer cards are dealt face up. This variation was once common but is rarely spread today.

Draw card: The card that a player receives when he either hits or doubles down.

Early surrender: The option of turning in your cards and giving up half of your bet before the dealer checks his hole card.

First base: The first seat or position at the blackjack table, to the dealer's left.

Flat bet: To bet the same amount on every hand.

Hard total: The total of a hand that either contains no aces or in which an ace must be counted as one.

Heads-up play: Playing alone against the dealer.

Hit: To receive another card.

Hole card: The dealer's downcard.

Insurance: A side bet wagering that the dealer has a 10-value card down, or a blackjack, when his upcard is an ace. Insurance pays 2-to-1.

Late surrender: The option of turning in your cards and giving up half of your bet after the dealer checks his hole card.

Marker: A casino check or draft used by a player to draw chips against his credit line.

Multideck game: A blackjack game in which more than one deck of cards is in play.

Natural: A blackjack.

Paint: A face card.

Pat hand: A hand that totals from 17 through 21.

Penetration: The number of cards that the house (or dealer) deals, on average, from a deck or shoe. The more cards that are dealt, the better it is for a card counter. But it makes no difference to the basic strategy player.

Pit boss: The casino supervisor in charge of a particular group of blackjack tables.

Point count system: A method of counting cards in which each rank is assigned a value when it is put into play.

Push: A tie. No money changes hands.

Rich: Said of a deck of cards or a shoe that has a disproportionate number of either high or low cards remaining.

Running count: The cumulative (count) value of all cards put into play.

Shoe: A device used to hold four or more decks of cards.

Shoe game: A game of blackjack in which the cards are dealt from a shoe.

Single-deck game: A blackjack game in which only one deck of cards is in play.

Snapper: Another name for a blackjack.

Soft hand: A hand that always contains an ace and therefore can have two totals. For example, ace-six can be counted as either 7 or 17.

Soft 17 rule: A rule stating that the casino must hit (as opposed to standing) on soft 17. This rule increases the house advantage by 0.20 percent.

Split: To make two separate hands from the original two cards. Only pairs and face cards may be split.

Stand: To not draw any cards.

Stiff: A hand that totals from 12 through 16.

Third base: The last seat or position at the blackjack table, to the dealer's right.

Toke: A tip.

True count: The running count divided by the number of decks remaining in a shoe.

Recommended Reading

The purpose of this booklet is to provide you with basic information for playing the casino game of blackjack. It is not designed to make you an expert player. Mastering this popular game requires an enormous amount of study, coupled with a great deal of practice both at and away from the "21" tables. This process can be accelerated, however, by absorbing the information available in a number of excellent blackjack books. In fact, should you become a serious student of the game, you will find the few books that follow essential to your success.

- *Beat the Dealer* by Edward O. Thorp, Ph.D.

- *Blackbelt in Blackjack* by Arnold Snyder

- *Million Dollar Blackjack* by Ken Uston

- *Basic Blackjack* by Stanford Wong

- *Professional Blackjack* by Stanford Wong

- *Blackjack Secrets* by Stanford Wong

- *The Theory of Blackjack* by Peter A. Griffin

- *Blackjack Essays* by Mason Malmuth

- *Fundamentals of Blackjack* by Carlson Chambliss and Thomas Roginski

- *Knock-Out Blackjack* by Olaf Vancura, Ph.D. and Ken Fuchs

- *Burning the Tables in Las Vegas* by Ian Andersen

- *Blackjack Attack 2000* by Don Schlesinger

66 Fundamentals of "21"

- *On Casino Gambling* by Darwin Ortiz

- Arnold Snyder's *Blackjack Forum* magazine

Index